WANTED

One Family

A TRUE STORY BY
Deanna Edwards

Artwork and cover design by Douglass Cole, Quantum Advertising
Text design and typesetting by L. Jane Clayson

❧

Library of Congress Catalog Card Number: 97-077979

ISBN: 0-9649968-4-7

❧

Printed in the United States of America

10 9 8 7 6 5 4 3 2 1

To all who have looked upon the face of
loneliness and found room at the inn
this book is dedicated

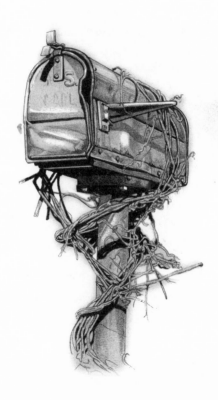

I feel privileged to have shared a journey of seventeen years with a lonely man who had the courage to reach out for love. His name is Joe Smarzik, and this is his story.

Deanna Edwards

Ice Storms

It was a cold winter in Minnesota. The ice storms began in October and never stopped. Walnut Grove had been hit especially hard. Snow covered the countryside, burying the fields, leaning in uneven drifts against the wood-framed houses. Grain elevators rose above the railroad tracks running the length of the small village. Barns and silos were silhouetted against the vast expanse of farmlands. The banks of Plum Creek were piled high with blankets of white snow. Christmas lights peeked through frosted windows, but one house was dimly lit. The curtains were tightly drawn, and a single lamp glowed through a yellowed shade. No matter how cold the temperature got outside, nothing could be colder than the loneliness of the old man within.

Joe Smarzik sat in an overstuffed chair, his eyes fixed on a distant past. A grandfather clock stood behind his chair, its oak frame laced with a striking silver pattern. Suspended in time, the hands on the clock were not moving anymore. They were just "there," not keeping time, just keeping Joe company.

It was a modest room, its corners filled with second-hand furniture. A calendar hung crookedly by the kitchen door, and a few old frames with faded pictures decorated the walls. If there was a treasure to be found in the room, it was the antique glass window in the door that led to the front porch. A delicately beautiful scene had been etched into the glass by the hand of a skilled artisan. Joe guessed the glass window must have been imported from Europe, since he had never seen another like it. There was a meadow, trees with intricately carved leaves, and, more importantly, a woman in the glass. She would appear only faintly in the evening lamplight, but by morning the sun rising from the east would strike the window and the woman would appear to come alive. She moved in ever-changing prisms of light, and her hair flowed about her face as if tossed by some mysterious breeze. Sometimes the woman in the window reminded Joe of his mother. At other times she was the image of Francis. Tonight he remembered both as he surveyed the landscape of his life.

Off in the distance he could see his Polish parents who immigrated to the United States before their six children were born. Eventually they settled in Minnesota in the areas of Walnut Grove and Tracy. His father was a railroad man with stern convictions about his responsibilities. Work was the measure of the man in the old country, and he firmly established these values in his children. His most sacred duty was putting a roof overhead and food on the table. Joe's mother worked hard too. She melted snow for the children's weekly baths in an old tin tub and baked bread and cakes that were the stuff of legends. She sewed the clothes her children wore and patiently stitched fine patterns in the quilts that covered their beds.

As homesteaders they depended heavily on the land to sustain them. Crops were planted and then harvested for canning, and the children would gather wild berries and hazelnuts in the woods. Anything edible was a precious commodity.

Before the heavy snows came, Joe's father made the long trip into town with his team of horses and a wagon to be loaded with enough sugar and flour to last the winter. He also bought apples and bags of candy for the children.

At Christmas time his dad would hitch up the horses to the bobsled. Straw was piled neatly inside. His mother would warm smooth flat rocks in the oven, place them on the straw, and cover them with blankets. The children were toasty warm as they went for rides amidst the beauty of frosty winters.

Joe's family could not afford to buy ornaments for the tree. They spent hours stringing popcorn and cranberries and making paper chains. It was a tradition he passed on to his own children.

Joe smiled as he remembered his little son and two small daughters. Trudging through the snowy woods, they would search for the perfect tree and excitedly help to pull it home. Once the tree was properly placed in front of their window, they turned it into their own Christmas fantasy with ornaments they had made themselves. Of course each year the tree was proclaimed to be more beautiful than the last. His wife, Francis, placed the nativity under the tree every year. The baby Jesus was never laid in the manger until Christmas Eve. The children, dressed in flannel pajamas, loved to lie on their backs, their eyes dancing in the glow of lights that were hiding in the branches. After they had gone to bed, their stockings were filled with oranges, banana-flip candies, and nuts.

When Joe was a child, his parents always spoke Polish in the home. He started first grade, unable to speak a word of English. The isolation produced by that language barrier proved to have far-reaching consequences in his life. He had difficulty fitting in with other kids. This was probably why he dropped out of school in sixth grade and went to work in a grocery store for two dollars a week. By the time he had learned to speak English effectively, he had become withdrawn and shy.

Years later a young woman with auburn hair, Francis Hardwick, danced her way into his life, coaxing him out of his shell and showering him with new life. They married and had three beautiful children. But as the years went by, Joe spent very little time with his family because of the long hours he worked. "I love you" was hard for him to say.

While Francis dreamed of discovering violets on a forest floor, traveling to distant lands, and making new friends, Joe longed for the familiarity of home, putting down roots and saving their money. He never refused any jobs and found great pleasure in doing them well. Their divorce didn't happen overnight. They tried time and again to make their marriage work. But one day she was gone, and the children were gone with her. How he missed them. Gone also were the reasons to celebrate Christmas or any other holiday for that matter.

Joe managed to fill his days with activity. He made trips to the sale barns and took pride in finding good bargains. He bought old homes, fixed them up, and sold them for much more than he paid. But the nights were hard, especially during the holidays. The happy sounds of laughter and conversation had long since been swallowed up in the vacuum of loneliness. The only footsteps to be heard in the small house were his own. For almost thirty years he had eaten a simple supper and retreated to his rocking chair, staring at a television screen he rarely turned on. There was always too much time to think about the past, wondering what might have been if his family had stayed together. Joe was beginning to realize that their unspoken agreement to withhold forgiveness from each other had not been worth the infinite silence.

Joe longed for one more Christmas to watch Francis in her busy preparations and the children excitedly opening their presents on Christmas morning. He couldn't face another Christmas alone. Maybe his own family was gone, but there had to be someone out there who could put the love back into Christmas.

He got up from his chair and rummaged through the top drawer of an antique desk that was bulging with accumulated odds and ends. Finding a pen and a pad of paper, he sat down to write a want ad that would change his life forever. It read, "WANTED: ONE FAMILY TO EAT CHRISTMAS DINNER WITH. I WILL FURNISH THE TURKEY."

The Want Ad

When Joe woke up the following morning, he felt the crisp cold air against his face. He hoped the pipes hadn't frozen as he pushed the bed covers aside, buried his feet in old woolen slippers, and hurried to turn up the furnace. He got dressed, remembering the years Francis had washed his shirts and trousers. If there was one chore he hated, it was doing his own laundry. The growing pile of soiled clothes in the hamper was a grim reminder of living alone.

Joe shuffled into the small kitchen to prepare his morning meal, glancing with satisfaction at the oak cabinets above the sink. He had built them himself when he remodeled the house. He reached in and pulled out some unmatched dishes, placing them carefully on the table next to a vase of plastic flowers. Slipping a napkin under the fork, he turned to the task of making breakfast. He had been eating alone for more years than he cared to remember, but he always carried out the ritual of meal preparation with unremitting dignity. Fresh food had to be properly cooked and served even if there was only one place set at the table.

The kitchen was soon filled with the aroma of his favorite breakfast—fried bacon and eggs and liberally buttered toast. As he sat down to eat, he glanced up at a painting on the wall. The old man in the picture was his only companion. He had a full white beard and thinning hair. His hands were clasped tightly against his wrinkled forehead, and he was bending over to bless a loaf of bread and a bowl of soup. His glasses were neatly folded on a big book Joe guessed was the Bible. Joe strongly identified with that picture. He admired, almost envied, the man's faith. But it was hard to pray over a meal he had to eat alone. There was something sacred about breaking bread with people you loved, people who loved you.

After finishing his breakfast Joe picked up the notepad he had written on the night before. He took one last look at it and stuffed it into his pocket. He disliked going out in below-freezing temperatures, but even more he dreaded the thought of another solitary Christmas. He had no close friends in town. At least in a newspaper he could maintain his anonymity. The empty years had taken their toll on Joe's heart. The wall built around it was as thick and solid as a block of ice, hiding the warmth deep inside. He found it difficult now to step outside his isolation and, perhaps, expose himself to more hurt, but he'd already decided to take the risk.

He put on his worn brown coat, pulled on his boots, and tucked his favorite tweed hat over his ears. As he stepped out onto his front porch, he was astonished at how high the snow had drifted, especially on the south side of the house. The snow had been blown nearly to the tops of the windows.

The sun was deceptively bright, but the air was unbearably cold. Joe drew his collar tight around his neck and began shoveling a path to his old pickup. The door creaked as he turned the handle and tugged on it. Sliding beneath the wheel, he wondered if it would start in the bitter cold. He felt a sense of relief as the engine caught and sputtered to life. Making his way cautiously out of the driveway, he drove slowly down the road, past the grain elevators, toward the neighboring town of Tracy. He parked in front of the *Tracy Headlight Herald* newspaper office and resolutely went inside. A young girl at the desk cheerfully took the ad and promised it would appear in the newspaper's want-ad section within a couple of days.

As Joe drove back toward Walnut Grove, he wondered if he had done the right thing. Who would be reading want ads with Christmas just around the corner? Would anyone see it? And if they did, would anyone call?

That night, Joe sat up later than usual in his old rocker. When he finally went to bed, he tossed and turned, fearful of what might happen when his want ad appeared in the newspaper. For the next couple of days, he could think of little else. Even when he was busy with chores, his mind drifted. At times he found himself staring out the window, gripping the arms of his chair with his big hands, waiting for someone to call.

On the day the want ad came out, the silence was broken by his ringing telephone. Joe reached for the phone, wondering if it would be the response he had been yearning for.

An Angel's Hand

*I*f help was ever needed in Tracy or nearby communities, people knew they could call on Homer Dobson. He never turned away anyone in need. He had been the pastor of his church for thirty-seven years. When he and his wife, Betty, had moved into the quiet neighborhood with its quaint tree-lined streets, they felt they had come to a place they could call home.

The Dobsons were deeply devoted to each other. Betty's quiet acts of kindness were a great support to her husband's ministry. Homer had a wide smile and a well of humor that bubbled up from deep within his soul. The tall handsome man was a contrast to his petite blue-eyed sweetheart. They always put up their decorations together because Homer could reach places Betty could not, setting a star atop the Christmas tree and lights in the highest branches. This Christmas Betty had been working in the kitchen baking star-shaped sugar cookies and gingerbread men. Their son Tom had already sampled more than his share of them. Gifts had been lovingly wrapped and placed beneath the tree. Carols were playing softly. The spirit of the season permeated the Dobson home from the basement to the chimney. Members of the congregation and good friends had been dropping by for days, bearing loaves of freshly baked bread, jars of cranberry jelly, and homemade ornaments to hang on the tree.

In a glass cabinet by their front door, myriads of angels stood on the shelves—some with wings of stained glass and others of porcelain. Along the hallways pictures of angels in antique frames smiled on every visitor. Betty had collected them over a period of many years. She and Homer had purchased the angels from antique stores, garage sales, and auctions. Her favorites were the pictures of guardian angels watching over little children.

As Betty prepared lunch in the kitchen, Homer picked up the *Tracy Headlight Herald* and settled back into his comfortable high-backed sofa. The glow from the lamp fell softly on his silver hair and face, illuminating the page in front of him. It was Homer's favorite place to read. By force of habit he turned to the want-ad section. He was always checking nearby farm and auction sales to see if they could find another guardian angel to add to Betty's treasured collection.

His eyes were drawn to an ad that stood out as if it had been underlined by an angel's hand: Joe's want ad.

For a moment it took Homer's breath away. The simplicity of the words stripped away a mask used to conceal a quiet desperation. Someone had placed a want ad to be loved.

He called to Betty. "Honey, there is something in the newspaper I'd like you to read."

The Innkeeper from Tracy

*J*oe's hand trembled as he answered the telephone. A deep resonant voice said, "Hello, I'm Pastor Homer Dobson. I saw your want ad in the paper today. My wife, Betty, and I would be honored if you'd join us for Christmas dinner."

These words shattered Joe's impression that no one cared. For what seemed like an eternity, he had been waiting for such an invitation. Now that it was just a voice away, he was almost speechless. Joe struggled to reply, "Thank you very much, Pastor Dobson. I'd love to come and have dinner with you and your family."

"Call me Homer. And don't bring the turkey. Just bring your appetite," he laughed. "My wife is a wonderful cook. We'll be eating about two PM, but come any time and stay as long as you'd like."

Joe suddenly felt vulnerable and afraid. He sensed a possibility of friendship in Homer's voice, but could he dare trust again? Believe again? He had grown crusty and pessimistic during his years alone. Would anyone be able to look past all of that and see the softness in his heart?

Christmas day came quickly. Joe nervously checked the closet to decide what to wear for this special occasion. He picked out a long-sleeved white shirt, a red-striped tie, and his best gray suit. As he laid his clothes across the sagging bed, doubts began to creep into his mind. Maybe it would be easier to cook his own dinner than go to the home of someone he had never met. He didn't want anyone feeling sorry for him. He hated pity. Understanding was okay, but not pity.

He forced himself into his best clothes, still filled with reservations. He put on his coat and hat and walked toward his truck. The sky was clear. The frozen snow crackled beneath his feet. Driving past snow-covered fields, he carefully followed the directions Homer had given him. As he approached the Dobson's home, he saw a little A-frame church right next to it with tall windows and wooden shingles. He would have coasted to a stop in front of Homer's house, but he couldn't convince his foot to press against the brakes. He just kept on driving.

He drove slowly around the block, feeling like a war was being waged inside him. His spirit wanted to go into the house, but his body wanted to beat a hasty retreat. It took several more trips around the block before he managed to stop. He sat in his truck, holding tightly to the steering wheel for a long while before he could muster the courage to open the door. Finally he got out and slowly walked up the snowy path and rang the doorbell.

When the door opened, Homer stood there grinning broadly, "Welcome to our home, Joe. We're so happy you could join us."

Joe crossed the threshold into the heart of the Dobson family's Christmas celebration. His eyes were first drawn to the white lace cloth that covered the big mahogany table. The table had been set with elegant china dishes like the ones that had belonged to his grandmother. The centerpiece was a golden brown turkey on a large oval platter. Betty had spared no effort at making this Christmas dinner extraordinary. There was stuffing, cranberry sauce, mashed potatoes, and pumpkin pie decorated with ribbons of whipped cream. A wonderful fragrance filled the room.

After taking their places at the table, everyone joined hands as Homer offered a heartfelt blessing on the food. Joe's fear was forgotten in the touch of someone's hand and the intimacy of the conversation and laughter that followed.

"This dinner reminds me of the ones my mother cooked when I was a child," he said with nostalgia. "She was from Poland, and many of her recipes were from the old country."

"What was your favorite?" asked Betty, refilling Joe's cup with hot apple cider.

"I liked her rice pudding. It had a blend of spices I've experimented with but never succeeded in duplicating. But this pie you made is wonderful. I've never tasted better."

"I love her cooking too," Homer added with enthusiasm. "Betty doesn't like leftovers, so don't be afraid to have seconds."

After dinner Joe carefully folded and replaced his linen napkin, studying the kind faces of the people who had rescued him from the silent void of another lonely Christmas. The meal was a feast fit for a king, but even better than the food was eating it with new friends.

In the midst of the celebration, Joe felt a familiar sadness tugging at the corner of his heart as he thought of his own family and the Christmases they had shared. But his pain was overshadowed by the experience of being with a family again. Christmas carols began to drift back into his heart, and the sight of their son Tom playing with his new electric train made Joe smile.

The Greatest Friend

After sharing that Christmas with Joe, Homer carried the want ad in his wallet. It had deeply affected his life and ministry. He and Betty had always provided a refuge for people in need, but Joe's want ad caused him to rededicate himself and open the door of his heart even wider. It brought more sharply into focus another Joseph and his wife, Mary, who had sought refuge at an inn two thousand years before. He wanted to do his best to be a modern-day innkeeper. He wished to more completely understand the needs of people who were suffering from loneliness and isolation. The want ad was Joe's

Christmas gift to Homer, and he never wanted to lose sight of the power of its message.

One day Homer learned that a visitor had come to Southwestern Minnesota who was singing songs of hope and comfort to elderly and dying patients in hospitals and nursing homes. An enthusiastic member of his congregation had heard her sing in the nearby town of Marshall and suggested that she be invited to perform at their church in Tracy.

Homer was intrigued with the idea of combining music with a ministry of healing. After numerous calls he was finally able to locate Deanna Edwards. He asked her to share her message with the members of his church and community. She agreed to come on a Sunday evening, accepting his invitation to stay in his home. "Not many motels around here," Homer explained.

On the night of the program, Deanna was dropped off directly in front of the church with her guitar, a big suitcase, and a heart full of the songs she had written. Homer graciously welcomed her into the quaint little church with arches that joined together to form the walls and a high ceiling. A stained-glass window caught the fading rays of the sun, reflecting a rainbow of colors. Above the altar hung a cross of pinewood.

"What a lovely church," Deanna exclaimed with admiration.

"I made the cross myself," Homer revealed. He walked to the front of the church and turned on a switch. White lights burst from behind the cross, illuminating the entire chapel and its eighty-five-year-old, hand-carved wooden benches. "I also serve as a pastor in a couple of other nearby communities, but most of my ministry is centered here. Is this your first trip to Minnesota?"

"Goodness no," she explained. "I've been coming to little towns in Minnesota for years. I love the people here."

In the warmth of conversation that followed, Homer felt he had met a kindred spirit. He reached for his wallet and took out a faded piece of newspaper. "I've been carrying this for a very long time and thought you might like to read it."

Deanna stared at the want ad, trying to comprehend the full measure of its meaning. "WANTED: ONE FAMILY TO EAT CHRISTMAS DINNER WITH. I WILL FURNISH THE TURKEY."

"Who placed the ad?" she asked, her eyes moistening with tears.

"His name is Joe Smarzik. He lives alone not far from here."

"Did someone invite him to dinner?" she questioned, struggling to regain her composure.

"My wife and I did. He has joined us for Christmas dinner ever since."

Deanna was visibly moved by the want ad. "It won't be easy tonight singing over a lump in my throat," she whispered.

Homer moved forward to greet the people who were beginning to arrive from Tracy and surrounding communities. They were unpretentious and casually dressed. He shook their hands enthusiastically, greeting most of them by their first names.

That night Homer's congregation joined Deanna in a musical journey into the human heart. She sang many of the songs she had written for people with special needs. When the program was over, there were hugs and expressions of gratitude as the church gradually emptied. Deanna picked up her guitar and placed it in the soft lining of the case. "Can you tell me more about the man who placed the want ad?" she asked Homer. "I just keep thinking about him and the courage it must have taken to do what he did."

"Well . . . when Joe placed the ad in the paper, he was doing what very few people in life do, especially with strangers. He was giving us a glimpse of how it feels to be alone. Evidently having no friends who were close enough to be aware of his need, he felt compelled to put an ad in the paper, telling our community what loneliness is all about—how it can hurt and how it robs us of the greatest things in life.

"How many times have we passed lonely people on the streets while we were busy shopping or buying groceries for Christmas dinner? We may glance their way and say, 'Merry Christmas,' but what does 'Merry Christmas' mean to someone whose heart is breaking? Christmas is about the coming of God's Only

Begotten Son to be the greatest friend known to mankind. But he can only be a friend to others through our lives."

A Song for Joe

Deanna stared out the window of the plane on her way to Atlanta, Georgia, to speak to a group of health care professionals. While some of the passengers buried their heads in the latest news and others drifted off to sleep, she was lost in the magic of the panorama outside. Today the earth was not visible at all. The clouds appeared to be towering peaks with deep hidden valleys. Here and there pale blue shadows stirred the imagination, allowing her to climb the mountain slopes with her eyes. While spring burst forth far beneath the clouds, above the earth it seemed more like a cold and frosty morning. The scene reminded her of the cold winters of Minnesota and the want ad Homer had shared with her.

It had been seven months since she had seen the ad, but the idea for a song had been planted firmly in her mind. She began to imagine what her response might have been if she had been the first to discover it. Music and words started to come to her. She reached down into the travel bag beneath her seat, pulled out a notebook and pen, and began to write. Her thoughts were filled with that first Christmas Eve—the night Joseph and Mary arrived in Bethlehem. After being turned away many times, they found refuge in a cave-like dwelling where animals were sheltered. In that humble stable the powers of all earthly kingdoms and empires were eclipsed by a baby with soft skin, newly opened eyes, and tiny hands waving to explore the world. This Child was the greatest gift of all.

When the wheels touched down in Atlanta, Joe's song was complete.

Several days later Deanna arrived home. She decided to stop and visit her sister Lydia, who was usually one of the first to hear her new songs. After she played Joe's song, she noticed tears in the eyes of her tender-hearted sister. "We need one more song for the album we are preparing to record in Nashville. Do you think this is the one?"

Unable to speak, Lydia nodded her approval. Suddenly Deanna noticed another person in the room. Lydia's ten-year-old daughter, Debbie, a blue-eyed child with a mop of yellow curls, had been listening intently from the doorway. She had a hurt expression in her eyes. "Can you go back and find that old man?" she pleaded. "Maybe I could write him a letter, and then he wouldn't be so lonely any more."

Return to Walnut Grove

As Homer Dobson sat in his study preparing his Sunday sermon, the phone rang. He heard Deanna's cheerful voice, "Homer, I'll be returning to Minnesota soon and wondered if I might come back and do another program in your church."

"Of course!" he exclaimed, happily surprised. "We'd love to hear from you again."

"But there are two conditions," she bargained. "The first is that I have the opportunity to meet Joe Smarzik, and the second is that I spend some time alone with him."

Homer agreed. When Deanna arrived, Joe was waiting at the entrance to the church. He was short and stocky, dressed in a dark suit, and wearing a reticent smile on his face. There were wisps of white hair about his neck and ears. The rest of his hair had vanished long ago.

Deanna could feel the excitement rising within her. Writing a song was one thing, but coming face-to-face with its inspiration was quite another. She felt compelled to meet the man who had reached out in an attempt to change his isolated existence. Though the want ad had been discovered in the farmlands of Minnesota, its message existed in the hearts of millions throughout the world.

Deanna greeted Joe warmly and introduced herself. "Homer told me about your want ad, Joe. I was deeply touched by it and felt inspired to write a song. Would you like to hear it?"

"No one has ever written a song for me before." His words were precise, spoken with a slight Polish accent.

They entered the church and found a small room next to the chapel. Deanna wanted Joe to hear the

song for the first time privately rather than in a room full of people. It was a moment to be shared with him alone.

"Joe, as I was singing your song to my sister, her little daughter Debbie asked me to come back and find you so she could write to you."

Joe smiled broadly at the thought. "I'll look forward to hearing from her."

Deanna took her guitar from the case, sat down and sang Joe's song:

WANTED: ONE FAMILY

On a cold and frosty morning
I picked up the local paper
And read the ads to pass the time away.
The radio was playing my favorite Christmas music,
Preparing for a special holiday.
The snow was falling quietly,
And a distant bell was calling me.
Through bitter cold such warmth was coming through,
And then, so unexpectedly,
These words were looking back at me,
And I felt as if my heart would break in two.

Wanted: one family to share my Christmas day.
Wanted: one friend to take the loneliness away.
I'm not asking much of you.
I'll only stay an hour or two.
I'll even bring the turkey if you call.

It's been a long and lonely day
Since I have watched a child at play,
And children are the greatest gifts of all.

The Christmas story filled my mind
And the night when Joseph couldn't find
One room for little Jesus to be born,
So in a manger filled with hay
The King of Kings was gently laid,
And angels sang for joy that Christmas morn.
My own Dad died in early spring,
And I couldn't help remembering
How much my children missed their Grandpa's love.
With trembling hands I took the phone,
Called the local nursing home,
And found the dear old man who wrote these words:

Wanted: one family to share my Christmas day.
Wanted: one friend to take the loneliness away.
I'm not asking much of you.
I'll only stay an hour or two.
I'll even bring the turkey if you call.

It's been a long and lonely day
Since I have watched a child at play,
And children are the greatest gifts of all.

"Thank you," he whispered, removing his glasses. He bowed his head, rubbed a gnarled hand over the few remaining strands of hair, and wiped tears away with the other.

After a long pause, Deanna asked, "Joe, why did you put the want ad in the paper?"

"Because people are so busy," he muttered. "The way it is today the younger ones just get too caught up with their own lives to think about folks like me."

In the stillness of the room a silent question formed in her consciousness. "Is there a difference between loving someone and paying attention to them?"

As she stood that evening to give her performance, Deanna noticed that Joe had chosen to sit inconspicuously in a corner at the back of the church. She looked at him intently for a moment and smiled. Then, turning to her audience, she began.

"Some people think that love can start and stop or begin and end, but I believe love is without a beginning and without an end. Some people think you can 'fall' in love but you don't 'fall.' You wake up to the beauty in another person and walk in the sunlight of your own awareness. Some people think you can 'fall out' of love, but you don't 'fall out.' You fall asleep. And when somebody falls into a deep sleep, they don't talk to you or touch you or hug you, and they can't see you anymore because they are busy dreaming about other things. But when you wake up to love for someone it's like watching a brilliant sunrise full of many colors. Suddenly the other person sees you and touches you with a sense of wonder, and listens to everything you say . . . and you never get tired when you are in the presence of love."

The following morning Deanna paid a visit to Joe. They sat on the front steps of his home in the shade of a tall maple and talked like two old friends. He told her stories about his life and places where he had lived and worked. It was too painful for him to talk about his family, so he shared with her what it was like to live alone. "You know it's harder to be alone in the winter when I can't leave the house much and there's not enough work to keep me busy. Minnesota winters are so cold most people just stay home."

Joe's elbows rested comfortably on his knees, his hands clasped in front of him. "I never thought my ad would lead to a song," he said in quiet contemplation.

"What you did, Joe, will help us all to be more sensitive to the needs of others," Deanna responded. "I'm sure there are many people who are reluctant to reach out when they feel isolated, but I'm glad you weren't afraid."

An Avalanche

of Love

*A*s the Christmas season drew near, Deanna's new album was distributed to radio stations, and many of them began to play "Wanted: One Family." A disk jockey at a local station played the song so much he began to receive inquiries. People wanted to know the story behind the song. One day he issued an appeal during his program: "Our station has received so many calls about this song I would love to locate Deanna Edwards. If anyone knows where she is, please call our station."

Deanna was busy preparing a meal for her family when she heard the request on the radio. She smiled to herself as she put aside her dinner preparations, dried her hands, and picked up the phone. Within minutes she was talking to him. "Ask and ye shall receive," she said, laughing.

"I didn't expect such a swift response," exclaimed the announcer. "I was not even aware you lived near here. Could you come in tomorrow afternoon—anytime during my show?"

Deanna tucked Joe's address into her purse before driving to the radio station. As the program began she told Joe's story to a wide listening audience. She concluded the interview by saying, "Joe would be very grateful if you could make this a Christmas to remember. I'd like everyone within the sound of my voice to find a pen and paper. I am going to give you Joe's address and hope you will send him a card, letter, a batch of cookies, or anything you like." Similar interviews on radio and television stations in other states followed.

Within a short time Joe's mailbox filled to legendary proportions. Deanna received an article from the *Tracy Headlight Herald*, showing Joe carrying his

mail to the house in buckets. The headline read: "SMARZIK FLOODED WITH LETTERS, CARDS FROM CHRISTMAS RECORDING".

Joe Smarzik has been getting so much mail lately he doesn't know if he'll ever have time to answer it. It all started with a want ad he placed in the *Headlight Herald* about five years ago.

"I never dreamed of anything like this," Smarzik told the *Herald* last week. "It makes you feel pretty good. I feel happy to have so many people responding to something like that. I don't know how to express my thanks."

Of the hundreds of letters that came pouring in, Joe especially loved the letters sent to him by children. Lydia's daughter, Debbie, had already become Joe's first pen pal. Deanna's youngest son, Eric, wrote, "Dear Joe, I'm thankful you have brought so much joy to others who need it. You have brought me so much. It's awesome your idea for putting the want ad in the paper . . . that you did that. Love, Eric."

Among Joe's favorites were letters from third graders in an elementary school in Ogden, Utah.

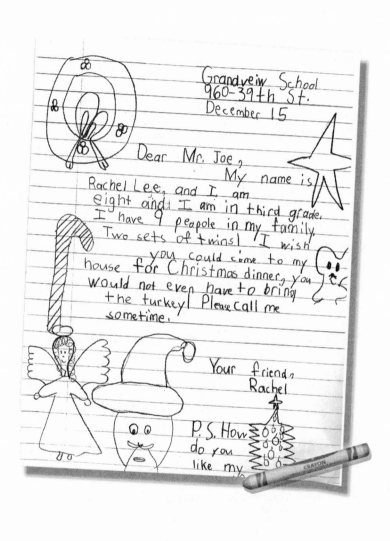

Grandveiw School
960-39th St.
December 15

Dear Mr. Joe,
              My name is
Rachel Lee, and I am
eight and I am in third grade,
I have 9 peapole in my family,
Two sets of twins! I wish
        you could come to my
house for Christmas dinner, you
would not even have to bring
the turkey! Please call me
sometime.

              Your friend,
                   Rachel

P.S. How
do you
like my

"Dear Mr. Joe, you could come to my house for Christmas and you would not have to bring the turkey and you would get the most presents. Love, Takara."

"I would let you come over and you don't have to bring anything at all. You would have to be willing to go on a six-hour trip though. We go to my grandma's for Christmas. Danielle."

"You could come and have dinner with me any night," wrote Melinda. "I'm eight years old. I'm not going to tell you how old my mom and dad are 'cause they would get mad."

An executive from a major Las Vegas hotel chain wrote to Joe: "Should your travels bring you to Las Vegas, please stop by and be our guest for lunch and dinner. We'd love to give you a room to stay a couple of nights."

One dear lady wrote, "Please know that you are in our hearts and minds always, and we love you—so now you have more relatives to add to your growing list. God bless you and watch over you."

One day Joe went to the mail box and saw a big white envelope. The address read, "The White

House, Washington, D.C." It contained a kind letter, holiday greetings from President Ronald Reagan and his wife, Nancy. A beautiful color portrait of the President and his wife was in the envelope, and both had autographed the picture.

As his house filled with mail and his life filled with friends, new photographs began to appear on the walls of his living room. Dressers and tables were crowded with each additional card or photo. No matter how time consuming, Joe tried to send a personal response to every letter he received. He was anxious to meet some of the people who had made such a dramatic impact in his life.

Friendship's Journey

The display of friendship that resulted from Joe's want ad was like opening a flood gate between those who are desperate to receive love and those who have a longing to give it. Wanting to become a part of the spirit of his message, leaders of various faiths began to have community dinners in church basements, inviting people of all ages to come and enjoy the fellowship of friends. Individuals began to look around their neighborhoods to see if there was someone like Joe they could help. Many people in nursing homes were welcomed into the lives of those who wanted to adopt a grandma or grandpa.

As his life was brightened daily by cards and calls, Joe continued to search for a way to thank the people who had responded to him. He decided to take a journey that would eventually span thousands of miles so he could express appreciation personally. At age eighty-seven, Joe packed his old pickup truck with clothes, some of his treasures, and bags of candy for children. He checked his wallet to make sure he had his driver's license and enough money to last several weeks. He bought a little white travel journal to record the places and people he would visit and set out on a four-hundred-mile-a-day mission. His trip took him to South Dakota, Colorado, Wyoming, Utah, and other western states.

The Anderson family from Wyoming were like Joe's second family. They had visited him on several occasions, and the six Anderson children loved him like a grandfather. Their home was his first stop along the way. They were overjoyed to see him and astonished at the long distance he had traveled to get there. He next went to see a family in Denver. They had been corresponding with Joe for five years.

He spent Easter with Deanna, her husband, Cliff, and their four sons in Provo, Utah. They dyed Easter eggs and filled baskets with eggs and candy, including some brought in from Joe's truck. Joe himself was given a basket overflowing with fruit and chocolates. "That's the first Easter basket I ever got," he said holding it almost reverently.

"Joe, we hide the kid's baskets every year in unlikely places around the house. Would you like to help us?" asked Deanna.

Joe chuckled at the thought of playing a joke on one of Cliff and Deanna's sons. Since Jeff's basket did not have a big handle, he was able to slide it easily under the sofa. With the exception of the Easter Sunday service, Joe made himself at home on the exact part of the sofa under which he had hidden Jeff's basket. Everyone laughed heartily when afternoon came and the hiding place was finally revealed.

Deanna, amazed that Joe would set off by himself on such a pilgrimage, sought to share his experience with as many people as possible. Upon learning of his arrival, more than a hundred people came to see him at an open house at the Edwards' home. Radio and television stations arranged for interviews.

Joe made it to his destinations, leaving a string of newspaper headlines behind him:

"LONELY MAN'S AD INSPIRED SINGER," heralded front page headlines in the *Minneapolis Sunday Tribune*.

"NEW-FOUND FRIENDS EASE LONELINESS FOR TRACY MAN," announced *The Independent* in Marshall, Minnesota.

"SONG CHANGES THE LIFE OF A ONCE LONELY MAN," declared the *Argus Leader* in Sioux Falls, South Dakota.

"A MAN'S PLEA OPENED A WORLD OF GENEROSITY: 87-YEAR-OLD'S WANT AD 10 YEARS AGO SEEKING A FAMILY FOR CHRISTMAS STILL GENERATES LOVE," reported the *Deseret News* in Salt Lake City, Utah.

In the *Ogden Standard Examiner* Joe's story appeared on the front page with the headline "GUEST IS COMING TO DINNER."

While in Ogden, Utah, Joe had decided to visit the Grandview Elementary school to thank the third graders who had written to him. The children's teacher was surprised to receive a call telling her Joe was in town and would be coming that very morning. The children were beside themselves with joy. "My students loved writing their letters to Mr. Joe, but we didn't think we would ever hear from you," said their teacher as she greeted Deanna and Joe at the door.

Though many children had written to Joe and he had responded to them, this was the first time he had an opportunity to visit them in person. He showed them where he lived on a big map of the United States that hung on the classroom wall and pointed out the highways he had traveled in his journey. He also told them that their letters had made him very happy and brightened his Christmas. When lunch time came he happily squeezed into a small desk and ate corn dogs and orange slices with the children as they excitedly asked him questions. To them he was a hero.

"I'm happy you're here Joe," exclaimed one little girl. "I wrote to you and said I felt sad because you were so lonely. I just wanted to make you happy."

"I wanted to make you feel loved," chimed in a small boy. "I don't know you very well but I heard a lot of stories about you."

"I think you are very brave driving from Minnesota to Ogden," said Jared. "How did you drive all that way without getting lost?"

"Well, you know that map I showed you? I had a small one like it in my truck and just followed it here."

An administrator at the school wrote in Joe's travel journal, "Dear Joe, thank you for visiting our school. It was such a pleasure to meet you. I keep your picture on the office door. A child asked me if you were my husband. Everyone in the office laughed and teased me about it."

As Joe began his journey home, he had intended to drive from Provo to Salt Lake City and from there to Interstate 80 East. Joe drove past his exit and several hours later discovered himself in southern Idaho before he decided to stop and ask for directions.

"Where am I?" he asked a service station attendant.

"You're in Pocatello, Idaho, sir," replied the young man.

Upon his return to Salt Lake City, Joe finally found his exit, chagrined that he had driven a few hundred miles out of his way. His trip back to Minnesota would be a very long one indeed.

Safely back in Walnut Grove, Joe read and reread the articles from newspapers that charted his journey. One of his favorites, written by JoAnn Jacobsen Wells, appeared on the front page of the *Deseret News* in Salt Lake City:

It takes a lot of good-natured prodding to get Joe Smarzik to smile. Even the slightest smile is quickly drowned in tears that stream down his cheeks when he hears the song, "Wanted: One Family," a song that ended forty years of loneliness and, this week, brought the native Minnesotan to Utah.

It was time, Joe felt, to say "thank you" to the hundreds of people who adopted him, sight unseen, after hearing the song.

Life for Joe Smarzik was never the same again. Seemingly overnight he became the grandpa that children had longed for, the missing father that busy women are never too busy to bake cookies for and much more. Joe became a symbol of hope for so many people who feel loneliness and isolation but never dare to put want ads in the paper.

Although he's read and reread each letter, Joe quit trying to answer them all. Instead he set out to say "thank you" in person.

"I came to say thank you," he said, opening his guest book for each friend to sign. "And to extend an invitation. If anyone comes to visit me, you are welcome to stay in my home."

Joe says he will furnish the turkey.

Heart Attack

There was one thing Joe found irresistible. He couldn't turn away from a good deal. The lure of the sale barns and auctions yielded enormous bargains as small farms went under or as people died or moved away. The population of Walnut Grove dwindled to only six hundred residents, and neighboring Tracy went from three to two thousand. The sagging economy prevented many of the young people from finding work, making it impossible to remain on the farmlands they loved. Many of the farm houses were put up for auction. It wasn't just the good prices, however, that drew Joe to the sales. It was the rich, musty smell of the barns, the sight of fresh fruits and vegetables, with beets and onions still clinging to long green leaves. It was pitchforks and ropes thrown up on the walls and the rugged, sunburned faces of the farmers who stood side by side with Joe in wordless fellowship.

One fateful summer day a sale was taking place in the nearby town of Sleighton. Joe drove his truck to the auction, got out, and went to look over the merchandise as he always did, but this time something was wrong. He didn't feel well. He reluctantly went back to his pickup, climbed in, and lay down on the seat. The temperature was in the eighties, compounded by Minnesota's smothering humidity. "Maybe it's just the heat," Joe reasoned, as he struggled to get his breath. But the longer he lay there, the worse he felt. He began to feel a tightening in his chest as sweat gathered on his brow and trickled down his face. He didn't want to bother anyone at the sale, but he began to sense he was in serious trouble. With great effort he managed to pull himself up behind the wheel of his truck and start the engine.

Joe knew where the Sleighton hospital was and prayed he would be able to make it there in time.

At the hospital, he parked outside the emergency room. It was a struggle to get out of his truck. The pain in his chest had become unbearable. He staggered through the entrance and collapsed. Joe didn't remember anything after the gathering darkness and the fading sound of voices. He didn't recall being taken to a small room and rolled onto a bed or hearing the nurse ask who they could call.

His worn leather wallet revealed a folded piece of paper inside that provided the information the nurse needed. As she unfolded it she saw the name "JoAnn" and a telephone number. The phone rang several times before the nurse heard a woman's voice: "This is JoAnn."

"A Mr. Joe Smarzik has just been admitted to our Sleighton Hospital emergency room, and we found your number in his wallet."

"He's my father," JoAnn exclaimed, a feeling gripping her heart she had not felt for many years. "What's wrong?" she asked in a worried voice.

"We think your father has suffered a heart attack."

"I'm on my way." she exclaimed.

A doctor came in to examine Joe. "Mr. Smarzik," he said, "you have congestive heart failure. We are going to admit you to the hospital for tests."

Joe mumbled an acknowledgment and drifted off to sleep. When he opened his eyes, the daughter he had not seen for almost forty years was sitting by his side.

"I'm here, Dad," she whispered.

A Daughter Comes Home

After receiving the call from the hospital, JoAnn sat for a moment in disbelief. The father she had been separated from for so many years was lying in a hospital in critical condition. Their relationship had been a rocky one. Childhood memories were few. He was often away, working so many different jobs she could not recall them all. The expression of sensitive emotions had always been hard for her dad. He seemed distant. How she had longed to hear the words, "I love you." She remembered the difficult struggle of her parents to stay together, until finally their different needs and personalities pulled them apart.

JoAnn quickly packed a few belongings and began the long drive from Verndale, Minnesota, to Sleighton. Her mind went back to one of her most beautiful but painful memories: her wedding day. The happy occasion was marred only by the absence of her father. She had written, asking him to walk her down the aisle and give her away. She waited a long time for his reply. To her dismay Joe declined the invitation. Unfortunately he was not able to share the struggle that was going on inside him. The separation from his wife and family had been too traumatic. He wanted very much to attend JoAnn's wedding, but he just couldn't find it within himself to go. JoAnn did not understand the deep sense of loss Joe would feel in facing his family. His refusal to come meant only one thing to her: her father did not love her.

But now, envisioning her father lying powerless and vulnerable in a hospital bed fighting for his life, she felt an urgency to reach out one more time, before it was too late.

Upon her arrival at the hospital she went straight to his room. He lay there sleeping, looking much older than she had imagined. In that moment she decided all the things that had divided them in the past didn't matter any more. She had only one father. He was a partner in giving her life, and they were forever a part of each other. No matter what his reaction, she would become the loving daughter he had missed for so many years.

Daffodils in the Snow

When Joe recovered from his coronary and returned home, it was with a warning from the doctor that he would have to change his lifestyle and avoid any heavy lifting or strenuous activity. Joe had never viewed himself as having any limitations. Now he would have to slow down. He was assisted by a new presence in his home. She had short curly auburn hair, a sweet smile and enough energy to make his head spin.

"Dad, how many years has it been since you washed your shirts?" JoAnn chided as she breezed by him with a basket of clothes. Though he didn't acknowledge it, he secretly appreciated the smell of the clean sheets she had washed and hung out to dry.

Joe felt it had been easier to drive clear across the country than it would be to steer through the clogged pathways that led to his daughter's heart. Both had been carrying grudges for so long it was hard to let go of them.

JoAnn periodically made the five-hour drive from Verndale to Walnut Grove. Joe began to notice a difference . . . the aroma of delicious meals that he did not have to prepare, the company of someone just being there. The corners of the house became cleaner and the cupboards brighter. He began to feel the comfort of her presence. The barrier between them was weakening.

The slow progress of rebuilding their relationship was frustrating for JoAnn. For one thing Joe was never satisfied with short visits. He felt family members needed time together. They had to spend leisurely hours with him in order to understand his world. JoAnn discovered that the key to restoring a relationship with her father was consistency. Even when her father retreated into the distrust of the past, she continued to come and visit him. Through quiet acts of service, she gradually overcame her own need for affirmation and reached out to reassure Joe that she was not going to go away, no matter what.

Sometimes Joe was gruff, but tender feelings were beginning to blossom in his heart like daffodils pushing up through melting Minnesota snows.

Joe still could not find a way to put his feelings into words when JoAnn came to visit. But often, when it came time for her to leave, she could see the tears brimming over in his eyes. Reassuring him that she would return, JoAnn was beginning to see "I love you" in her father's tears.

The Grandson

*I*f ever there was a gift of the heart to Joe, it was Myron. He was the grandson Joe had always dreamed about. Myron's smile was contagious as it danced above his broad chin. Both were proud of the striking resemblance they bore to each other.

Joe was the grandfather Myron had never known but had always missed. His keen insights and deep spiritual understanding of his grandfather were almost startling; he was able to recognize his grandfather's faith.

Their relationship began after Joe's heart attack. When Myron became aware he had a grandfather

ᛞ

living only a few hours from his home in Minnesota, he was overjoyed. He had accompanied his wife Pam many times to the home of her grandparents. She was devoted to them and found great delight in the love they felt for each other. Myron had quietly watched the meaningful interactions between them and wished he had a grandparent with whom to share his life. He wanted to pass that heritage to his children. Part of his identity was missing, and he knew that he would be able to learn more about himself through coming to know and love his grandfather.

This quest was easier for Myron than for his mother, JoAnn. He came into the relationship un-encumbered by painful memories of the past. He had made no judgments and drawn no conclusions about the character of his grandfather. Though the hour was late in Joe's life, Myron was writing a new story. He realized that the members of his grandfather's family had all been looking through different windows, each seeing a different view. Myron knew that healing was possible only through forgiveness. He sought more to understand than to be understood, more to love than to be loved. And there was much to learn from his grandfather. Joe had lived nearly one hundred years, and Myron wanted to look into the treasure chest of his life and come to know what Joe could teach him. He accepted Joe just as he was.

Myron had fond memories of another great teacher, his Grandma Smarzik. Unlike Grandpa Smarzik, Francis made a decision to leave Walnut Grove. She traveled throughout the world and came back with exotic stories from Alaska to Africa to tell her grandchildren. She would invite them to her home one at a time to teach them and take them for nature walks past the fence rows that divided the farms and into the woods to look for colorful rocks, identifying species of wild flowers and other plants along the way.

Now it was time to build memories with Joe. When Joe got out his briefcase containing the treasured articles of his adventures across the country, Myron listened with both interest and respect. He read letters from people who had adopted Joe and discovered the need for love that had prompted him to put his want ad in the paper. But Myron's greatest joy was to watch his four children, Tiffany, Trever, Tyler, and Tabatha, winning over Joe's heart, invading his privacy, leaving a trail of toys in his house, and climbing on his knees to say, "I love you, grandpa." "Great grandpa" was much too difficult for a little child to say. Through the interactions with the children, he began to watch his real grandfather emerge.

Joe related stories to Myron, sharing his experiences in the ice business before refrigerators were invented, telling about his hot dog stand in Omaha, and explaining how he had gone from managing a restaurant to owning an antique furniture store.

He passed his years of knowledge on to Myron, teaching him to tie a load so it would not shift on a truck and how to hook up and tow a disabled vehicle. He showed him how to tell if an old house was worth buying by checking the foundation for cracks, looking for water spots and evidence of other kinds of damage. Joe taught him that restoration would be easy if the foundation was strong.

Mealtimes were of utmost importance to Joe. Whenever Myron's family came to dinner, Joe would not touch his food until everyone was present. Each week he would take Myron, Pam, and the children out to dinner at the MED Club in Tracy, a favorite eating establishment. Gradually, with the consistency of the family coming to visit, feelings began to deepen and love began to grow. The missing puzzle pieces in Myron's heart, and in Joe's, began to fall into place.

Myron and Pam decided to move to Walnut Grove to be close to their grandfather. Joe owned a house only four doors down from his and sold it to Myron at a price not to be refused. It was a stately white house with a beautiful red maple tree in the front yard. The house needed fixing up, and soon the sound of hammers and saws could be heard as Myron and his family began to remodel it under the watchful eyes of Grandpa Smarzik. Myron began to suspect that one reason Joe had purchased houses in the area was to provide a home for any family member who wanted to come and live in Walnut Grove.

Myron witnessed a remarkable evolution in his grandfather's life. Joe went from being a man who counted every nickel to one who was generous in every aspect of his life. The curtains in Joe's house were opened wide to let in the sunlight, doors were opened to let in the fresh air, and gallons of ice cream were scooped up and offered in cones to children all around the neighborhood. Companionship was becoming a daily blessing in Joe's life and in the lives of those who knew him.

The Reunion

*J*oe was ninety-two years old. Unknown to his family, he had always kept track of his children. Even when they thought he didn't care, deep in his heart he loved and missed them. He had old photographs and newspaper articles hidden away, yellowed with age, that preserved his family's history.

Life had changed so much for him since beloved family members had come back into his life that when his daughter JoAnn suggested a family reunion Joe was thrilled with the idea. A family reunion was an event he had always yearned for.

Even JoAnn was surprised as she watched her father throw his energy into the preparations. For the weekend event Joe had planned a catered meal at the MED Club. He personally secured tickets for all to see the famous outdoor pageant, "Fragments of a Dream." Residents of Walnut Grove were proud that the renowned author Laura Ingalls Wilder had once lived there. The production featured stories from her book *Little House on the Prairie*.

JoAnn had baked hundreds of cookies for the reunion. She also had cleaned not only her father's home but the other places where family members would stay. She and her husband had made a number of florescent orange signs that said, "SMARZIK–HARDWICK FAMILY REUNION," inviting relatives of both Joe and Francis. They wanted to make sure no one got lost on their way to the dinner, the outdoor play, or the picnic in the park where games and other activities had been planned. JoAnn's husband was both loving and playful as he cleaned his father-in-law's yard, ran errands, and planned ways to drench everyone with water balloons.

What surprised the family most were the old photographs, some dating back into the early 1900s, that seemed to appear from nowhere in Joe's home. He stored them all in a big gray suitcase. Deanna, who had been invited to come and provide the entertainment, was enlisted to help Joe and JoAnn label the pictures of family members with as many names and dates as could be recalled. They were all to be displayed at the reunion. It was fascinating to see the handsome photos of Joe as a young man and the pictures of his parent's fiftieth wedding anniversary.

As everyone worked, more grandchildren and great-grandchildren began to fill the house. Little hands were reaching to sample the cookies, and soon Joe's small kitchen became a scene of happy chaos. In the midst of it all, Myron and Pam, carrying little Tabatha, burst in to inform everyone that beds had been freshly made.

Those who could not come to the reunion were there in heart and spirit. Joe's son had remained in North Carolina where he and his wife were caring for her elderly mother. Joe's oldest daughter, a nurse from Massachusetts, had cared for Francis during the final years of her life. Unable to attend the reunion, she sent a large bouquet of red carnations and white daisies.

The following day the reunion unfolded in the beauty of a Minnesota summer. Sun sparkled on acres of corn, turning rows of graceful leaves into waves of silver. Joe's family and friends happily followed the bright orange signs directing the way to the Smarzik–Hardwick reunion, down Highway 14 to the MED Club. Long tables had been set up in the banquet hall. Homer Dobson had been invited to be the master of ceremonies. As he welcomed everyone, he observed the happy scene and remembered the once-lonely man who had shared Christmas dinners at his table.

When JoAnn stood, she looked lovingly at all who had come to unite in a celebration of new relationships. It was an emotional moment for her. Looking now at her family, she felt a deep sense of gratitude that they were together again. As the festivities began, JoAnn passed out special prizes to those who had come the greatest distance and to the oldest and the youngest persons in attendance. She expressed appreciation that Deanna had come to join them for this special occasion.

When Deanna sang she felt an old familiar lump in her throat, not unlike the one she had felt when she first read Joe's want ad. But this time it was a lump of joy for an event she had been praying for. She sang familiar songs that everyone could sing with her. At the conclusion of the dinner, an accordion player began to play old-time music. Joe suddenly grabbed Deanna's hand and began to waltz her around the room. He had loved dancing all his life, and his steps were still smooth despite his 92 years.

It was a challenge to round up mischievous boys and girls and convince them to stand still long enough for family pictures to be taken. Soon all the children were gathered around Joe as cameras recorded the miracle of a family once divided coming together. Pride and contentment filled Joe's face as he surveyed the happy commotion.

The reunion was a resounding success. Remembrances had been shared. Most attending had been delighted by the pageant and thoroughly drenched by the water balloons. Now there would be new pictures in Joe's scrapbook, pictures of him surrounded by the family he loved. Joe had enjoyed the entire reunion, but the words that touched his heart most and that he had longed to hear for so many years, were "Dad" and "Grandpa."

After the activities of the reunion came to a close everyone gathered at Joe's house. Tired children were gathered up, and leftovers from the picnic were tucked into his refrigerator. The family had unspoken concerns about how Joe would feel when everyone left to return to their homes. Most of them said their goodbyes, leaving only Myron's family and Deanna.

Myron was hesitant about leaving his grandfather. He walked into the kitchen where Joe was sitting at the table, trying to accustom himself to the gathering silence. "Want to play a game, Grandpa?" he asked.

Joe's face brightened. Tiffany came to play the game of Pinochle as Deanna joined in. Pam attended to little Tabatha, whose round face and mischievous smile were much like her great grandfather's. Tyler and Trever played outside, discovering more hiding places in Joe's yard.

Soon Myron had to gather up his family for the long drive home. He was looking forward to the time when the house they were remodeling would be ready for them to move into so they could be closer to Joe.

After they had gone, Deanna could see a great sadness in Joe's eyes. In an effort to break the silence, she asked, "Would you like some supper?"

She prepared a simple meal of bread and hot soup. They sat down at the table together. Joe, who was sitting beneath the picture of the old man praying, bowed his head. He began to offer a simple blessing on the food. Deanna was deeply moved. It was the first time she had ever heard Joe pray.

Before leaving Minnesota she gave an emotional performance at the church where she had first met Joe. Retracing the steps that brought her to Tracy, she wondered if this would be the last time she would see Joe sitting quietly behind the others.

That evening Deanna stayed with Homer and Betty. The following morning they drove her to the airport in Sioux Falls. She expressed concern for Joe, and all agreed to call him that day to find out how he was feeling. Deanna called him from the airport, but there was no answer. Homer and Betty also called

Joe's home and received no response. When Deanna returned to her home, she called Joe again. When he did not answer, she called Homer and Betty. "He looked so tired last night," she said in a worried voice. "Do you think the exertion of the reunion wore him out. Could the heat and activities have caused another heart attack?" She was close to tears.

"Not to worry," said Homer. "I'll check it out."

He called the police, and an officer went over to inspect Joe's house, while Deanna called JoAnn in Verndale. In no time Joe's voice was on the line. "What are you doing checking up on me?" he asked, heartily amused at the concern in her voice.

"Joe, we've been trying to reach you all day. Homer, Betty, and I have been so anxious about you."

Joe laughed. "I got lonesome for the kids and decided to come and see them. We've been playing games and having a great time."

Because Joe had experienced having his family around him, he did not want to endure another lonely day without them.

A Lasting Legacy

It was Christmas again in Walnut Grove. Snow was falling softly on tree branches and covering the ground. The house Joe Smarzik lived in was sparkling with joy, and gifts were piled beneath the tree Myron and Pam had helped him decorate. When the children came in to open their presents, Joe delighted in watching their happy faces. The true beauty of Christmas, Joe realized, was the children. They filled his life with love just as his own children had many Christmases before.

Suddenly Tiffany began to cry. Her brother had mischievously thrown her new doll across the room.

Tiffany yelled, "I don't want to play with you ever again!" and ran to Joe for comfort.

Joe gathered her close, pressed his weathered cheek against her soft hair, and whispered, "You know, honey, a long time ago Grandpa got his feelings hurt and let pride come between him and the love of his family. Now that you are in my life, Tiffany, I realize the terrible price we all paid. So many years have been lost when we could have been together. Family members often say and do things that are hurtful, but they should never forget that deep down inside, they love each other. So, honey, you must forgive your brothers when they break your toys or hurt your feelings. You can learn to overlook all that, but you can never learn to live without love."

After thinking about what her great-grandfather had said, Tiffany jumped from his lap and went back to play with her brother. Joe looked out at the falling snow. A group of carolers were singing in the distance, "Silent night, holy night, all is calm, all is bright." These words had greater meaning to Joe than ever before. He looked at Tiffany with great tenderness. He knew he had just shared with her an everlasting gift: the legacy of love and the power of forgiveness. Now Joe was no longer the guest in need. He was the innkeeper, and there were many rooms in his heart.

Anyone wishing to send greetings to Joe
may write him at the following address:

Joe Smarzik
P.O. Box C-74
Walnut Grove, MN 56180

Special Thanks to

My beloved husband, Cliff, and my children;

Joe Smarzik and his family, who allowed this story to be told;

My publisher, Stewart H. Beveridge, and his wife, Gaylyn, for believing;

My dear friend and favorite story teller, Marsha Cutler; and

Homer and Betty, who taught me that when there is love in the heart there is room at the inn.

About the Author

Deanna Edwards is an author, composer, singer, and humanitarian. She sings in sixteen languages, has written over two hundred songs, and has recorded one hundred of them on ten albums. She has dedicated her life to serving those in need. For many years her music, seminars, and personal visits have brought peace and comfort to the sick, elderly, and grieving throughout the world.

Deanna was named one of fifty American Heroines by *Ladies' Home Journal*. She and her husband, Cliff, are the parents of four sons.